Written by Sumal Ashfaq
Cover Illustration by Emma Marjorie Roberts

Copyright © 2021 Ripple Foundation
All rights reserved. No part of this publication may be reproduced in whole or in part, by any means without permissionof the publisher of this book.
For information, please email info@ripplefoundation.ca

ISBN: 979-8523131578
Published by Ripple Foundation
Visit our website www.ripplefoundation.ca
First print edition 2021

TABLE OF CONTENT

The Power of Words 1

Ink and Paper 2

The Sound of Colour 3

Stars Aglow 5

Home 6

Blended 7

The Power Inside Me 8

A Hundred Stories 9

Heart Made of Ink 10

A Flower 12

Lady of the Lake 13

Shhh 15

Living 16

Up Above 17

Lullaby 18

You Have it All 19

My Words 20

Goodnight 22

Inky Universe 23

Never Gone 24

Ripple Foundation is a charitable organization that aims to empower the next generation of leaders by fostering creativity and cultivating a passion for reading and writing in youth across Canada.

Kids Write 4 Kids is an annual writing contest for youth in grades 4-8. The net proceeds from the book sales are donated to the winner's charity of choice. Our other programs include the Write It Workshops, a creative writing program designed to motivate young authors. The program focuses on improving the writing skills of children in grades 4-8. Participants are encouraged to find their voice and gain confidence in their choices and skills as a writer. The Wave Blog is an online publication for youth in grades 8-12 where they get to share their experiences and thoughts on topics relevant to them and their peers. This platform strives to increase the public's awareness of young authors and their voices.

Visit ripplefoundation.ca for more information.

ABOUT THE AUTHOR

Sumal Ashfaq is an eighth grader located in Southern Ontario. She's an aspiring writer and poet who loves exploring the vast world of storytelling. Sumal loves experimenting with different styles of literature and basking in the world of poetry. She also loves to capture her environment through drawings and paintings, filling out her many sketchbooks. When she's not exercising her creative muscles, Sumal can be found fangirling over a new book or excessively saving recipes to her Pinterest boards. As for her taste in books, she will literally read anything from the classics to fantasy although currently, she's reading many historical fictions. Sumal draws her inspiration from many authors such as Marissa Meyer, Alan Gratz, Abbie Emmons, and Kimberley Bradeley. She is forever grateful for the constant support from her family, friends, teachers, and twin sister. You can find Sumal on her Instagram page @thatlefthandedartist.

The Power of Words

Our words hold power

stronger than magic itself

swirling on the page.

Ink and Paper

The paper
never crumpled or curled
as she set the ink down.

It stayed still for her words
absorbing the emotion
that she sent its way
and with every dip of ink
and every stroke of the pen
the paper obeyed.

Resulting in a poem
worth putting on display.

The Sound of Colour

thud
He drops the tubes of paint
Onto the desk.

squish
He squirts the cobalt blue
onto his rainbow
palette.

swish
Goes the water
as he cleans the soft bristles of the brush
twirling them
in the cup.

thunk
He drums his fingertips
on the table, waiting for inspiration
to hit.

gasp
An idea rushes to his head
and a sound of awe escapes to his
lips.

badump
The melody of the music
playing alongside his work
thrums in his ears
as he mixes his colours
one
by
one.

scrap
The palette knife scrapes the canvas
with the texture of the Earth.

hmmm
he breathes
as the colours come to life.

tap
His shoes hit the floor
as he steps back
and admires the blues and greens
creating a world of trees
captured on a sheet.

Stars Aglow

The stars don't complain,
they don't get tired of lighting
up our darkened world.

Home

Every house has a smell,
and when I breathe in
the air
I pretend
that I'm there.

I pretend that I am touching the walls
of my home.
I pretend that I'm smelling the food
that was baked all those years ago.
I pretend that I'm in the same room
living through a memory
I wish I could live through
once more.

But no amount of pretending
can bring back the place
I called home.

Blended

She blended her colors
in circular strokes
with a brush
that was shaped like the moon.

The green
bled into the blue
then touched the
yellow sun
and poured
into the white clouds,
uniting the lands
and the seas
as one.

The yellows, the greens and the blues
were a seamless gradient of hues
and values.

Like the sun spilling into the
sky and into
the sea.

The Power Inside Me
Magic flowed through her veins
thumping
and pumping,

   flooding her vessels
   like a volcano
   about to
   erupt.

      Like a wave
      crashing
      onto shore.

         The magic
         was the energy,
         the food,
         that fueled her soul.

            It hummed in her fingertips
            waiting
            to burst.

A Hundred Stories

The window was open
and the stars shined bright
as I got lost
in the world
of ink and paper.

I was no longer
in the comfort of my home
and instead,
familiar fairy tales
surrounded me.

Who needed an airplane ticket,
when I could
jump down rabbit holes,
battle Captain Hook,
and travel through
a wardrobe
to a magical world
without having to move
my feet?

Heart Made of Ink

She has a heart
made of ink
that pumps through her veins
like blood.

She bottles her emotions
and spills them
onto the page.

They cry,
they laugh,
they scream,
with joy when they read
the words
that she's written.

They beg for more
and she provides.

Until every single feeling
and emotion that ran through her mind
has said goodbye.

Then she is left alone
as empty as a
slate and
as hard as a
stone.

A Flower

The purple petals
contrast the yellow center,
stem growing upwards.

Lady of the Lake

Her hair was alive
and swayed in the breeze
swishing and swirling
creating a whirlpool
around her.

In the deepest depths
of her roots
and beyond
was a world only she knew of.

A world of creatures
that swam in the lake
filled with mermaids
and sailboats
of men
and fish.

A world that polluted her hair
and the lake inside,
the world inside.

A world
that turned her hair
green with envy
and brown with dirt.

And so,
the magical deep blue
of the lake attached to her
roots
no longer stayed
the colour of the sky.

Instead
resembled the ugly colour
of human greed.

Shhh

Shhh, the children are asleep,
dreaming in the dark of night.

Shhh, the children lie in bed,
caught in the movies of their minds.

Shhh, the children snore softly,
surrendering to the night.

Living

The forest was alive

only at night

when the humans said goodbye

and left nature to be right.

The animals came out of hiding,

and the trees began to sing.

Then the eerie night

turned loud

filled with beauty,

filled with life.

Up Above

Through the ancient trees
stars dot the inky sky and
the moon peeks through them.

Lullaby

Oh sweet sister of mine
let me sing you a lullaby.

Let me rock you in my arms
and shield you from the world.

Let me share with you the song
meant only for your ears.

Let me give you the love
that's always here.

Oh sweet sister of mine
fall asleep
and surrender to the night.

You Have it All
It doesn't matter
how tall you are
how strong you are
how grand you are
how beautiful you are.

The size of your house
and car
don't matter.

The amount
of clothes you own
and followers you have
don't matter.

Because
we are not the
weight of our
skin
or our clothes
we are the weight
of our body
and our soul.

My Words

What is this feeling
that makes me feel
so grand?

I can put every
thought
and every memory
right in front of me,
weaving together
intricate webs
of words and
creating lyrical
perfection.

I will
exaggerate,
agitate,
saturate,
and originate
every thought in a magical way.
I'll make people feel my
pain

and my excitement
as if they were
reading my mind.

All with the help
of letters strung together.
What a powerful thing
words are.

Goodnight

What a lovely world
it is when the humans
are asleep.

The moon covers the night sky
like a big orb of light
and the trees sing to the sky,
swaying in the wind.

The whole world is lulled
to a silent state.

So peaceful,
so calm.

I can't help but fall
asleep.

Inky Universe
The ink bottle
tipped over
spilling a universe
out onto
my desk.

Never Gone

When will you open your eyes
and look up at the stars?

When will you realize
that all the beauty you need
is right above you
waiting to be seen?

Millions and millions of stars
light up the night sky
glowing bright,
feeding off the beauty that surrounds them.

And even when they disappear,
blocked out by the glow of the sun,
they're still out there
providing light
to someone else
somewhere else.

But each night
They still return
To you
Providing you with the light

And the love
That had always been there
You had just refused to see it.

So now,
open your eyes and
open them wide.

Manufactured by Amazon.ca
Bolton, ON